BEARING MY SOUL TO HIM...

Untold soul conversations with the heavenly Father...

D . H . Deflorimonte

Volume #1

BEARING MY SOUL TO HIM…

Issued in print format.
ISBN: 978-1-9994116-2-6

Book Design & Special Effects Artist: By Destiny Deflorimonte

For more Information:
Instagram: destiny.dofficial

Psalms 102:9

"For he satisfies the longing soul, and filleth the
hungry soul with goodness."

BEARING MY SOUL TO HIM…

BEARING MY SOUL TO HIM...

Flawed caused story

I was created in the image of my creator, but I was completely different from him. I was made to possess his qualities and likeness, but it had seemed as though I could not quite live up to the expectation. You see this housing unit that he has placed me in was tampered with by sin. Yes, it was tampered with. Tampered in the sense that sin crept in and mutated the genetic coding to my substance. A virus it was. A virus that had become a widespread epidemic throughout the world. It was a deadly virus that killed me spiritually to the realization that Christ was the antidote to my long-suffering, pain like desire to be set free from these deathly shackles. I was alive in the sense that the virus named sin made my countenance likened unto a zombie. Living but not quite alive. That virus birthed in me its own antigens and materials that sprung up qualities that were not like my creator's. I roamed the earth like a crazed beast, looking for its next meal. Diseased, beastly, abominable, ugly, disgusting, abandon, unworthy of attention and love was my name; that sin had called me and more. To sin more was the word that was used as a whip against us on a continual daily basis that we have all become used to. Used to... Used to in the days that when sin was rampant within our bodies and we were burdened by its beckoning calls. Used to when sin would give the seconds of highs and the forever seemed like lows. Used to when sin used us and abused us by introducing feelings for within the acts, in wanting more. For more of the highs, more of the excitement, more of the body driven ecstasies called adrenaline. For more felt like the perfect eternity stamp for these moments. Used to, was something we have become used to by its routinely acts. Used to when we would try to convince ourselves that this would be the last time. Used to when we would try to clean ourselves up and could not. Used to is something I hate to have to admit but we have become used to... For, I am flawed because of one-act. An act that became likened unto a heart attack. Attack! It screamed as it attacked the spirit of everything. Disrupting the pattern of God's creation in its manner. All because of one-act... You have to see that I was not there nor was it me that committed such an act, but I do play just as much a part in this story of creation fallen from grace over this one sinful act. For I am a descendant of this act. For, I am the result of this act. But most of all, for, I am now made alive by the one who was there when this act was made. For he saw that I was flawed. For he knew me and was thinking about me when he died on that stake. For he knew the stakes and chose to demonstrate the father's love to a world that has plainly forsaken his love as not enough. For, I have to proclaim that his love is worthy of me for I am not worthy of his love. For if he can say, " I am a worm and no man;" and he is the creator, what am I? For I am nothing, without him. Yet he saw me amongst the billions of his creations and demonstrated that he wanted me more than anything that my little world could ever comprehend. I have to profess, that when he came walking in the cool of the day of my calamity, he called my true name. His voice and the name he was calling out were estranged to me but yet his voice was familiar and calming. My countenance shook and trembled like mount Horeb by the voice of my creator pursuing me. Then his eyes met mine. He spoke and broke the silence between space and time. And said, "it is by time that I had adopted you." For, I am flawed. What do you want to do with me? I am not worthy of your presence, nor love. I am not worthy of your thought of me, nor mercies. I am not worthy of tenderness, nor grace. I am not worthy of your adoption, nor bearing your name. I am not worthy to be called the apple of your eye, nor the person after your own heart. For, I am not worthy, because I am flawed. For then he says to me, "I love those who are flawed because my love oversees their flaws and they become unto perfection in me." "For, I am the author and finisher of your flawed story", "to put an end to your broken heart and worries." "For, I chose to die for those who came from the original flawed caused story."

BEARING MY SOUL TO HIM...

The one for me

The one for me. For he is the one for me. He is stronger than the men of this earth. His hands created everything including creativity and life itself. His voice is like many waters and thunder in twine together, as all men know that what he does, let no man put asunder. His voice pierces and electrifies the very DNA of who he speaks with. His arms are longer than life, as he tells those to let go of strife and to take sight of him. His embrace melts many and his love is full and plenty. His eyes are striking at the sight, yet shows true genuine love, tenderness, and care, which shines bright. His breath breathes life into everything it passes through and molds it, as he holds it in his hands. His nose delights in the sweet-smelling savor of men's worship. His forehead lines are caused by the many expressions he makes by watching man, go on blind without asking him. His lips speak the truth and the words that come forth are not void, as his words come knocking like Floyd. His face displays the emotion of pleasure, anguish, laughter, and sternness. His feet run full speed to those whom he seeks. Then I had found him pursuing me with those same feet. He gave us his only begotten son, of whom we chose to meet. For, I do not know what was in me to interest him. For, he knew me a thousand eternity lifetimes and yet he still wanted me. I never knew him, but deep-down words could not even describe this hidden secret bond we had. To me, I thought that I was your average joe-girl, for him to pursue me and tell me that I was completely otherwise. He showed me what true love was really about. He told me to trust in it, nor to doubt because he is the very author and creator of it. Love showed me the creator's heart and unearth like passion and depths that he holds. For he is the one for me. In times of soul-crushing trials, he calls my name and bears my burdens. For he is the one for me. For he heals my wounds and restoreth my soul when it is weary. For he restores the blind to see and makes the deaf to hear. For he is the one for me. For who can restore the soul as he can? For who can love wider and harder than he can? For who can walk with me through my trials and bear them all when I fall? For, I have not yet found such a one who can do this in all of the earth like him. For he is my comforter, deliver, rock, shield, creator, father, and friend. For I am won over by the one who created me and my story. To show those who read this of his glory, that he is the one for me. The one for me…

BEARING MY SOUL TO HIM...

The man who stole thine heart

I did not come unto to thee to perform this rhythmic melody, to show thee of my interests. Political, moral, views, nor thoughts; but to tell thee of the man who stole my heart. He not only captured my heart but my mind and bounded them both together. Neither does his voice escape this maze that life has molded within me. The first word that comes to mind of how I am towards him in our relationship, is how unfaithful I have been. Such a sin, but the real question should I pose; aren't we all are? Or have been? As you can see, there have been countless times that I've gone a strange and whoring over things, people, situations, relations, and more, which was depriving this man of my heart, mind, and body of what I've truly had in stored. This is all because I became momentarily bored with him and became occupied with the world's pearls, in which I had secretly stored within. Attention, oh no focus, oh no my heart, and more. And yet, still, he comes knocking at my door. You see, he looks through the windows and at times I find him sitting with his back against the door; calling for me, to accept the plea of being free and reborn. As you can see, I am not good, especially towards him. For I toy around with the man whose shoe latches I am not worthy of unlatching. For I let him stay in the home of my heart for but a while and kick him out for nothing he did wrong. As I kick him out due to the guilty song within my consciousness of how wrong I am. As I cheat on him with someone who is not him. For I am selfish, for I cheat on him with me. You have to understand that the characters of the " me, myself, and I" are one evil individual. As it is pretty literal and typical that it would seek for my destruction to be on the most pinnacle, of advantages. But this man's love comes with bandages, that manages to sandwich us between his sweet love. For my words do not do justice to his love, which comes from above. No earthly language, nor word can describe this type of love, for it leaves this unearth like humming; that keeps those who have tasted and are addicted to this loving coming. For he is the reason I exist today, as I obey to proclaim his love for me. For he is the reason I can think properly and can see. For he is the reason I wake up in the morning and can breathe. For he is the reason why there is a roof over my head and food within my belly. For he is the reason why I am called destiny and I am successful today. For he is the reason why I may have a life after death in his eternal bliss. For this is the man who stole my heart, but captured my mind and bounded them both together. As I said before that I did not come unto thee to perform this rhythmic melody to show thee of my interests, political, views, nor thoughts; but to tell thee of the man who stole this heart...

BEARING MY SOUL TO HIM...

The day of my calamity

"For how dare you take a life you can't even replace?" were the words that my creator spoke to me on the day that I had decided to take this life away and replace it with empty space. For it was my last year in elementary school and one month away from my eighth-grade graduation. For I did not want no "congratulations," nor that "you did so well"; for I was waiting for the perfect time to call it quits to this living hell. For I was in a fog that did not shed the light of day for a year. A fog that had fogged the man and woman of God's decerning of what was going on within their child and home. For, I had felt as though, I had clocked out of this fleshly home. So, I put Dorothy on and tapped my heels together and said the words, "there is no place like home," thinking that it would actually bring me back home. For which I remember that I am not Dorothy, for I actually have a God that can give me my heart's desires, nor do I need to tap my heels together in order for his head to turn; or to think that it is about time to bring me back home. But this time, it was something about this particular time that I had actually lost my mind and could not find my way out of it. For I felt lost, and could not boss the thought of actually seeking help in the day of my calamity; for my hands were too clammy and my teeth were too chattery. For, it felt as though I was on the other side watching life pass me by, with a smile saying goodbye finally. For now, I know what it means to be invisible and cynical, for when I had gone to church to actually seek for something a little bit more reasonable, they had told me to "not take this thing called life too literal." For how could you say something so detrimental to someone who's so brittle? For I felt belittled, breakable like a peanut brittle, hopeless like Israel, was a ghost-like invisible, so fed up with life miserable, alone and crazed fearful. For I was depressed and was on the verge to put this life on the hashtag "rest in peace life fam fast." for, I had actually played with the idea of seeing this player's life out for the entire season. For, I could not reason and had taken a bottle of something very so serious and had emptied it into my system. Then I heard a voice that was like many waters' and trillions of thunders and lightings, speak from within my being, electrifying every cell and coding of my DNA. Saying, "how dare you take a life you can not even replace!" "For your life is not yours to take!" For within that moment I had felt no greater fear and utmost regret and was sorry for my actions. "My daughter, for are you going to diminish all that I had planned for you?" For every word that he had spoken, it felt as though he was writing it upon the table stones of my heart. For he left me feeling like I had taken my first ever breath, in which I believe I was birthed into this next level savage. For my God birthed in me this savage that wanted to go out and salvage all that was taken from this new savage. For hope and grace was re-established for this savage to go on to the next advantage, to bring a disadvantage to those who thought that they were the real savages. For when the day of your calamity comes, I want you to have it set in your mind to be 1 chronicle 28:20 " be strong and of a good courage: fear not, nor be dismayed: for the lord god, even my god, will be with thee; he will not fail thee, nor forsake thee, until thou hast finished all the work, the work for the service of the house of the lord." For this is for those who have won, lost and has attempted during the battle of the day of their calamity. To be strong and of a good courage.

BEARING MY SOUL TO HIM…

The word

For words are just tools to use. For anyone can be a tool and sound like a fool. Words are like birds that can sore high or low and can even feel like a blow to any man's soul. For words can be rhymed like mine, as you can see that I am doing such a crime by the time. But in the most of things, words mean a lot and can leave any man with snot, rot, or caught. For words demonstrate and captivate the hearers that can only truly relate. For it took words to start the surge of creation. For within creation, it shows its intricate detail and dedication. For it did not need manipulation nor persuasion for the elements to move at the sound of the vibrations of the creator's voice. Which was moist than the waters that had covered the earth. For the famous three words started with "let there be," to start the motion that gave way to that one word that came with force like rough oceans. For he was that light in our night, to bring us of his delights. For he was the very word. For he came and wrapped himself in flesh, to die the most grotesque, to show us his utmost best, for us to follow in his familiar like tests and to be laid in his rest.   For he is the word and the word is him. Yet still to this day, they can't even comprehend. For they are not willing to be the clay and bend, as the potter desires to mend. For he stated in his very own words that he came here to not pretend but to lend us his heavenly heart again. For we are not worthy of such a man, nor to be able to hold his hand, for he says we can in the midst of our storm. For he knew the stakes and signed the form and became the most high's firstborn. For on the day and hour of this man's mourn, creation and time took a step back and was torn. For his stripes gave me pipes and his buffeting gave me toughening. For he is the very word. So now that when you go before his throne and he asks you, you cannot say that you never heard. For these words are and for him, so don't dismiss this, for in the day that you do so you will be solely pissed. For his name means everything and so often taken in vain. For his name is the word and the word is his name. For he is the, I am that I am, for all of this was in his plan; so that we could understand that he is the very word that stand.

True believer

The true believer does not need no lever nor a read to tell them of their God. For God is no bog in their equation nor relation, neither in their situation. For the true believer knows their master's voice and comes to him by choice. For they display attributes like a forgiving joseph, humble like Moses, courage like Joshua and Caleb, determined like Elijah, relentless like Jacob, faithful and loyal like job and a heart like David. For they carry their master's characteristics like logistics, to then be labeled as misfits by societies 'statistics. For the true believer knows that this type of living is not for the faint in hearted, in which the new beginners say, " oh darn it" and think twice of being departed. For the true believer knows all pressure is measured and can often feel like a desert. For they worship like David and raid the entire vision of the belated, in which they stated, "put back on your clothes David." Only the true believer has seen the vision that Christ has given and made it their mission to pursue what was mentioned. For the true believer knows their line of duty, for this, is their call of duty; for there is not time to chat nor to catch a snooze. In which I am sorry to be such a doozie. For this is not to be made the call of duty second, third, nor fourth; for you to get that this is the ultimate warfare. For we do not need to the calls, as we specialize in black ops and go on to the next level like it is hopscotch. For the true believer gets convicted for which the lord depicted when we would take on his name, inflicted. For the true believer knows what it means to be addicted and cannot be restricted, for they know they will not be evicted. For my question for you is, does what I had said make cents? For I am not a bank for you to cash out blank cheques nor to pay off your hidden debts, but to tell you that the lord is coming one day like a forgotten rent. For the true believer knows that saving their oil was not easy through their turmoil, while being in a world that is so hooked on the spoils. For they know what it truly means to be loyal, for they are taught by the very man who created and wrapped himself to be loyal. For the true believer knows the woes that the enemy sends out to your soul, that feels like a blow that can knock you off your toes and can leave any man feeling low. For they are placed on repeat, whenever they get knocked off of their feet; to stand and brush their clothes off. In which they are sent into a rage and go off and will not stop until they doze off. For the true believer knows how to praise, for they are not lazed like the rest who sit in their heavenly father's house of praise; looking dazed by those who routinely haze those who promote an idea of how to get of their maze. For the true believer knows when the master calls for all else must fall and to stand before him tall and to not have him be stalled. For when he comes are you going to be standing? For what he is demanding is for you to live the rest of your life hanging in his grace. For he is grace in this place that had no trace of race, nor face.

BEARING MY SOUL TO HIM...

Thine will be done

Oh lord take this cup from me, for I desire to do your will and not my will in and through me. For my will desires to be that kill bill type of will; for it desires not to be still and seeks for the thrill hill to have me killed. For I am not skilled to put this thing to rest, for which I come to you in all of my mess and confess to rid me of this pest. For you blessed me and gave me of your nest and laded my head on your chest; to then you tell me to not oppressed, for I am no longer a guest but a daughter for which you say, " let me do the rest, for I am an expert and can do my utmost best; in which I request one thing of you." "For I am going to put you on a quest to get the rest who are like you that are in the west, north, east, and south." "For this is what the kingdom of God is all about, so never doubt." "Nor get distressed for you will go through trials and test, to bring out the best in you; for I took out the less in you, so there isn't no stress on you." "For this is what my will is about." "You see, I had to sign the bill for you to get out; for this was the only way for me to kill that thing called doubt, for this is what mine and my father's will is about." "For the I am, that I am, loves you." "For this is all because of you, that I had to make sure that this very thing be revealed unto you." In which I respond, not my will abba, not mine. For I am not worthy of thine time, but it will be a pleasure of mine to know thee of the rest of my lifetime and to climb to know this ultimate prime. For, I do not care how others will look at me by doing this crime, for I am guilty. For my only plea is that you will come with me and that you will do thy will in and through me.

Holy

Holy do the angels cry on high, holy, holy, holy. For you went beyond measures to show me, that you were not phony and had told me words that had sold me to who you are. For your love gave me kisses ever so slowly liken unto a newborn child, who is fragile and vulnerable; for you know me. For I caught your eyes and you wanted me only for yourself, for you are holy and a jealous God. For we both had dreams of you holding me and slowly rocking me to sleep, in which you became my one and only hero. For your eyes were always on the sparrows and made sure I was on the straight and narrow. For you had told me that I will never be lonely, for he who has been called holy has molded me for this lifetime story. For I thank you for restoring me, for you will never be a bore to me; in which I pledge my life to say forever are you holy. For your love makes us shout holy moly, for it comes to us so boldly. For your words feeds us until we are roly-poly for your glory are, we are saying holy, holy, holy. So, when there is nothing left to say other than tears proclaiming how holy you are and what you have done for me. For you have rekindled a new type of fun in me. For all of your creation sings this song unto thee, holy, holy, holy is the lord God almighty. For you were the one that had told me words that had sold me to who you are holy.

For I desire to be amongst the ones who say holy, holy, holy and will patiently wait for you to call on this soldier home to glory.

BEARING MY SOUL TO HIM…

Habitation

For, I desire for you to be the invasion of this habitation, so I can become apart of your nation. For the population that is yours knows you. For you have become my education, in which I study you with dedication, for information to know all about you. For, I did not need, no persuasion nor any manipulation for you to become the invasion of this habitation. For it is known that of your reputation of staying within the homes of our hearts is not just for an occasion; to make plain conversation. For, I would gladly accept your invitation to go with you to your homely destination. For you did not need temptation to capture my heart to be apart of your equation, type of invasion. For you are my vacation and since I am apart of your creation, I will move at the sound of your vibration; for you are the navigation of this habitation. For there will be no hesitation from this habitation, in which I plea for you to take me with you on your next destination. For my life, body and will are your habitations, to make an invasion. For beyond creation, this was all in your plan, type of formation. For this is my rededication of this habitation to be apart of your soul-saving invasion.

BEARING MY SOUL TO HIM...

Hero

Before the creation of time and the days were numbered zero, you were destined to be my one and only hero. For you pursued me like a fast arrow and told me your way is the only straight and narrow. For you say do not worry about the sparrows for my eyes are always on the sparrows. For you may think that I am weird but the one who renamed me makes the coding of my bone marrow bow. For it is now that I vow unto, thou to plow through this thing called life to be able to make you say wow. For when I look back on my life, all I could say is how in which you remind me if you were not in the equation would I be able to come to this point; and say a somehow. For it is you that allow and disallow the things that go on in our life. For you are my hero, for you come in with a pow and knock all my enemies bow an arrows down. For you say, "don't look down," in which I put two and two together and find out that I could very well drown. For this is my enemies very well wish to go to town. For you smile and say, "oh my daughter, for it is now that you belong to my town, so look around and see that all that I have is thee." "For you and I had visions and dreams of I holding you and slowly rocking you to sleep, and I becoming your one and only hero." "Your god, creator, father, friend, and hero, is me; for I have and will always be a constant unto thee." "For you are apart of me and if I have to cross an eternity worth of seas to have you set free, then I would; for I am your hero and that is what I'll forever be unto thee."

BEARING MY SOUL TO HIM...

Take a knee

For, I will take a knee, to the one who has saved me and formed me. For the one who has put this life plan into motion, does not give me small portions of his love. For his love comes down from above, like a dove and diminishes all thereof and ingrains itself upon those who ask to be made fit to him like a glove. For I didn't need a shove to give him my knee nor my love, for it was me that I plea that I would live my life, not on the edge of a kind of nor a sort of; for I have found out that this is true love. For he died on a tree for me you see, as love was the key for him to overcome death so that we can be set free. It is now that I can see that you are my reality and if it takes this lifelong sea to know thee, then let it be. For you deserve more than just me and this world, for you treat us like pearls. I know that we have done things that have made you want to hurl and have your fists curled; for it is because we agree that we are flawed. For it may seem odd to those who have never seen nor heard of the cause. For, God deserves more than just my applause, for if I realize that and do not change; I would be a fraud, who has the most damning flaw about me. For if creation gives thee of their knee, so will I. For if my enemy has given to thee his knee to thee, then there should not be a pause from me; to give thee of my knee. For, you have formed me, and it is I who wants to be fit to you like a glove and will put you above all that I love.

BEARING MY SOUL TO HIM...

Diamonds

Shine bright like a diamond and I am not chiming Rihanna's rhythmic song diamond. For I am rhyming about the diamonds that my heavenly father creates, that comes out shining. Let me introduce you to his diamonds, for they go climbing to his designed assignments and come out roaring like lions. For his diamonds are purposely put through heated climates and pressure for some timing. Trying to find them is no different from gold mining. For everybody knows diamonds are known for their beauty and worth; for they are birthed within the earth, which is labeled God's turf. For they are bright like the shining light and blur the sight of those who were born in the night. For they were birthed by the one who brings us of his delights, at the speed of light. For the one who creates them is known to be that light that is brighter than white and whose height, depth, strength, and might are unknown. For he holds tight to his diamonds and never loses sight of them, because he keeps them close to his home(heart). For his diamonds fight with might to shine bright, to be able to reach higher heights in him; despite at times losing sight on him. For his diamonds unite and never fright at the sight of being called to a fight. For they are cut for this and do not need to be able to strut their stuff for this, to be able to stunt on this.

For what?! For you to feel this in the gut and be made shut to what was previously made cut deep? So, as I will repeat, for those who meet the description of his diamonds are told to shine bright. For he is coming one day like a thief in the night, to bring you to his heavenly home, which is more of than a delight, so shine bright.

BEARING MY SOUL TO HIM...

Calamity (part 2)

The day of my calamity, for it was a day that you could not quite get past me. For it was a tragedy that became my reality, for it was in my humanity that it held this secret insanity; that felt like a never-ending agony. For it was the day of my calamity when life ran pass me and all else went up like no gravity. Yes, it was depression. For it was birthed from aggression, stressing, and oppression; and it had taken of my reflection and had molded it into something that I couldn't quite get out to do a confession nor to come around to do any sort of expression. Any suggestion? For this was not a session nor a lesson on the direction in progression in possession. For I did not get any discretion when it came at me with all of its questions; for my only obsession and focus was to be made in his perfection. So, when it had seemed as though I never heard from him nor felt from him for an entire year; it felt as though I was amongst the rejection. For all of this was real and I could not feel anything. For, I had tried my utmost best to have the zeal to appeal what felt like a heavy-laden steel, and be made healed. For I did not get the option on this wheel of life to take the deal or no deal; for it to be revealed into my life. For this was a test on me in the day of my calamity. For it was like unto a shot to the chest to bring out the best in me. Now you can see the new me had no rest in me and screamed to go on to the new quest, you see. I now detest to be made waste in my nest of mess, you see; for I am too blessed to rest, you see. For I will invest all of my best for you to see, that anything coming from me is nothing less, you see. For I am more than blessed to stand here today to tell you of how I was depressed, for the one who made you and I is just more than a guess away; and is only requesting one thing, which is that you give him of your heart today.

BEARING MY SOUL TO HIM...

Abide

"Abide in me and I abide in you", were the words you spoke to me; for you to get through. For I had to hide because of my pride was too high like a tide and was being supplied by the one who occupied the genetic sinister side, of this fleshly home in which I reside. For I had moments in my flesh where I had cried and couldn't decide to be which bride you see and couldn't hide my disguise and had tried to die by burning the one who was on me like a leach; and found out that I too was being fried in the process. For, I was trying to live by a guide that had only pointed towards my graveside. Then you came to me by my side, giving me all that you supplied; asking me to really look inside, in which you advised that when I abide in you, that we would collide and bind. For which you say, "you are mine, you see. For I was the one who chose to die for mankind, for this was designed in the form that I had signed. For, I knew that I was going to be the one who was going to be left at the backs of everyone's minds. Being placed on a shelf that they create, to show me whenever they are reminded of me; and then to find me whenever they are blinded you see. For it was I who chose to abide in you, stronger than glue. For I wore the shoe for you to never see the view that you were predestined to, after the fall. For it was I who gave you my all, to take that which is small to stand tall and to call that which is a wall to fall. For I am the vine and thee are the branches. For I did not need chances nor no circumstances to come after you like a heavy-laden avalanche; to bring to you of my advantages. For don't you know that all of heaven dances when you become apart of me, as a tree with all of my branches. So, take refuge and abide in me, for there is no limit nor depth, nor sky in me; for I am too wide you see. For I am the alpha and the omega who died for thee, and who rose up again and now resides in thee. Remember the word that I had said to you, for if they persecute me then they will surely persecute you too. If they had kept my saying, they will keep yours as well; for I am the bell who is calling out to those to abide in me and dwell amongst those who excels. Now that ye are clean through the word that I have spoken unto you. Abide in me and I in you. As the branch cannot bear fruit of itself, except it abide in the tree; no more can ye, except ye abide in me."

BEARING MY SOUL TO HIM...

Princess

For when we as daughters of the night become adopted by the father of the light, we attain his delights with no "might". For he has sons who become princes and daughters who become princesses, but my question is, have you ever stopped to question why does the first letter (p) in princess looks so much like the (p) in process. For yes, it is one and its length is likened unto a game of chess in success, and its path is full of stress and big messes, that can often leave you feeling less than. For that was never the plan man, to feel less than who you were met to be. Can you see, for I might not be queen b, but I did come here to proclaim that "who the son sets free is free indeed." For Disney portrays this strange idolized way of being a true princess. Oh Disney, Disney, Disney. Isn't it sticky that the bible's version of how a woman should be, disses thee? For I do not need to wait for the clock to strike twelve to know that your slipper of a princess does not fit me so well. For I am not bell, for my beauty reflects my father who created me and sets me apart from those who dwell amongst the well of the beast. For I only feast from my father's hands of peace, truth, and love; for his drug makes you want to hug and to be made fit to him like a glove. For your word says for us to be either hot as red or cold-like blue, and to be not stuck in between the purple like stew. For if you had not rescued me, I too was going to die, and I did not need to prick my finger on a spinning wheel to see as to why. For I don't need a magic carpet for I have you to set me upon your wings of the morning to let me see any view that I desires' to; for my desires are plenty and no genie can help me. I vow to you that the only thing that I entangle myself with is nothing but your word; brushing through your word so that I can stand in any given demand. For I do not wish to trade places with a fish, for all they want is to be able to feel sand underneath their feet. For, I did not need to sign a form of deceit to be able to meet my desires of feeling complete. For I don't need to enlist myself as the opposite sex to be able to be in your army, for your requirements is to never be tardy and to never let the enemy disarm me; for their only mission is to swarm me and harm me. For this royalty will only intertwine these hands with loyalty and will never lock lips with frogs who were birthed from the father of dishonesty. So with formality, I will speak these words with originality, that I will only seek the one who has saved me and who has put a smile between these cheeks and will tweak the sound of the beat of my drum, with a unique sound that was instilled by the father. So as a daughter, I will bother the idea of being less than stronger and will carry on the title of being the king's daughter.

BEARING MY SOUL TO HIM...

Master

Master. For his mass is something I cannot comprehend; for it always leaves me to a deserted end. For his plan seems to never end in his hands of where greater stands. His arms are the comfiest place to land after walking amongst his days of earthly life on end. For he is always onto something grander and when he asks of anything, we will answer, humbly at the commander. For he is the master that comes graciously into our lives as the most amazing encounter, and diminish all that was negative with his power. For he is the lion, that comes out flying to devour the enemy's strong towers. For he is the master that goes through our pastures with a true genuine laughter, that will leave a plastered smile on our faces due to his amazing graces. For he is more than just a master or a pastor that screams to watch out for that disaster. For he is the shepherd that has the most outstanding record of holding the most demanding job of being the master and plaster that hold life stature together. It will be more than my pleasure here and now and hereafter, that I will be more than honored to pour my box of alabaster to the one true master who carries all of my answers in his chapters; and who renewed me as a new creature and has written me with a happily ever after. For he is the only master that should matter in this letter to you about the real master. So, I suggest to gather those who are desiring that love, laughter, and answer to what we have been looking for from here on after.

BEARING MY SOUL TO HIM...

24/7 connected with heaven

24/7 connected with heaven is what was mentioned in the saving grace redemption. A connection so strong, that it would make you want to throw away your gps, because of its connection that leads you to the direction; of the one who is dripping in the word of affection. Perfection is he who becomes apart of our being and is in twined with us, as you can see. He gave us of his injection that caused a reaction in us to be able to move with action; militant with our attention, swift with the discerning, strong with friction, took on his name infliction and was made alive again in his resurrection. So, with this 24/7 connected with heaven type of connection, it is nothing liken unto your wi-fi imperfections. For, this connection has its own reservations that will cause you to look at your own reflection to see if it matches with heaven's. Its reception is nothing short from fascination and a celebration. For this connection has the most greatest insurance of protection, that specializes in globalization. So, my question is, what is your connection and are you 24/7 connected with heaven?

BEARING MY SOUL TO HIM...

My beloved

My beloved, for he is unmoved. For my beloved is mine and I am his, for there is nothing extra to it because it just is. Oh, stay with me flagons, comfort me with apples, for I am sick with love. For his hands come to embrace with a hug, like a dove caring for its very own beloved. For all I ask is to let me hear your voice, for it is comely and is way above me and loves me; whispers in my ear that I will never be lonely. For my beloved did not just come suddenly, lovingly to me; for he always has, as he places me in his home. At thy mention of thy name, makes others want to spaz and foam. For my beloved, you have no spot nor wrinkle in thee, just a simple twinkle in your eye at the sight and mention of me. My beloved how is thy love better than wine and thy scent drips its greatness between space and time; for you are my beloved. For no man is more deserving of my time nor love, than thine. For my beloved, I will rhyme these rhythmic chimes unto thee for the rest of my lifetime; for you are the author and finisher of my story time. For my beloved, you are the sign that reminds me that I am not mine but thine. For my beloved spoke these words and said this just for you. "Rise up my love, my fair one, and come away with me. For lo the winter is past, and the rain has gone away. The flowers appear on the earth; the time of singing of birds has come. The voice of mine and my father's will is asking you to come and be won by the one who holds all earth, moon, and sun..." For my beloved is mine and I am his, for there is nothing to it because it just is, so now that I know that you are his beloved too as well. I guess it is about time to ring the beloved bell.

BEARING MY SOUL TO HIM...

The requested go

"I had said go. For no man knows the woes that I have gone through to show that I still love. I request that you throw your woes on me and grow in me and become lighter than snow in me. So, the enemy does not come again and be the cock that crows and slows that "go now, go " process unto thee. For he is the foe that owes everything to you and deserves every blow that is coming to his soul, you see. For his days of being sent below are coming soon when the moon shows you the gloom of the doom to him and his accomplices too. For I had said go and be the embryo that I know that grows and be overflown as a cup filled with new wine in me. I am asking you to go and allow me to floe in and through you, to let me be that light that shines bright unto your toes, you see. Even when you are feeling low, remember and know that you are stronger than any buffalo and let my presences rest upon your face; like what happened to Moses ages ago. For I am the husbandman that sowth his seeds and is expecting a harvest when I come to reap, with no weeds. For you are my seed and I am requesting you to go and be free and to succeed. For I will be more repetitive than any radio will ever be, as I ride through the waves with my father's rowboat on the morrow. So, to those who have ears, let them hear, for the father says not to fear but hold up your spears and to go into battle and shed your enemies' blood and tears."

BEARING MY SOUL TO HIM...

Dry bones

Dry bones. Were once thrones who held the leader of its home. Bones that once echoed groans and moans of the pain-stricken by sin, which you come to shed your blood on the cross to atone. Bones that once glistened like rhinestones before the fall to be fallen to the earth like rough stones. Bones that spoke of its lifetime and yet still speak the silence of dead phones. Oh Father, but when you speak, time itself peeks its ears to listen at the sound of thy lips; in order to repeat thy promise. For when you speak, it is louder than a million megaphones in which you call out amongst the tombstones unto these dry bones, to "come alive." For many will ask why, in which you reply. "For I am the one who is going to come inside to thrive in you and instill an unending drive in you." "So, go and tell them that you had once died and is now made alive, purposely revived for this day and time; by the one who defies human logic and sense of time." For it is he alone who decides that it is about time to call these dry bones alive, so let them make way for the father to come and say "a rise" to these dry bones; that were once made alive.

BEARING MY SOUL TO HIM...

The door knock

"Behold, I stand at the door and knock; if any many hear my voice, and open the door, I will come into him and I will sup with him, and he with me." 'knock, knock, knock,' for it is he who is asking you to unlock the door of thine heart before the tick-tock, clock stops, and time is no more. For I am the rock that you have been panting for and is asking you to just come with me for a walk and talk; in order that I can show you a life with more and more. For I am he who blocks the shock that the enemy sends out to your heart to stop. For behold, it is I who stands there, waiting, watching you debating if you should answer the door with a frustrating why; to the one who is willing to give both sun, moon, earth, and sky. For the time is fading, and I have not come here to ask if you have been misbehaving. For the home of your heart is breaking and I need for you to be evacuating. I am asking you to let me in to replace the hating with praying and the anticipating waiting with playing. For you have been asking when the celebrating will be in a world that is so hooked on the slaying and the decaying of others. I ask, that you allow me to operate in you to be the changing thing that causes the shaking difference in this world. For all I want is to be embracing you and to be creating a new thing in you. For it is I who is chasing you and is asking to let me come in, to rearrange your home to something new. For this is no negotiation, it is that you take my offer or will not have me waiting. So, my beloved, please open the door, for it is only I who can restoreth man's soul; for it is I who has come knocking at thine door forevermore. 'Knock, knock, knock.'

BEARING MY SOUL TO HIM...

Time

For they say time is money. And I do not think it is quite funny that my time is being robbed out from under me. For my time is costly and it would be a crime to spend it on things that dimes could pay for. For my time is worth more than this earthly currency, as one can plainly see. For my time in experiences, of being the creator's "witness" and climbing life's mountain called challenges have cost me and has brought me to gain. A product that has stained me forever. For within time, it holds these secret pleasures that are often thrown on the scale of being measured; by others who do not know its worth. For this chimed rhymed is not said in order that one to feel sublimed about this fixated lifetime with multiple pleasures. For I am just the messenger that was sent purposefully to deliver the package that is known to be sour. Sour to those who do not think twice about this fleshly home of which we reside; that it has its own expiration date and time. For it wouldn't be my fate to try to clean the grime of former men's ideology, of working hard on overtime for a slivered dime that neither worries about my length of days being spent on the grind for things, people, and situations that could care less of my wellbeing. Now that I have your attention, for the time being, one will now be able to hear the prewarning that the father will be ringing the bell for those who are willing to come dine with him until time has taken to the stand to be still.

BEARING MY SOUL TO HIM...

Raw

I am raw like my creator. Formed beautifully and wonderfully made in the image and likeness of him. Raw in the sense that I am merely fashioned in his exact composition, yet was created from the dust of the ground in which his words took to its purest form and created my material. As it is literal, go to the word to find this as biblical. For I am, composed of body, mind, consciousness, and soul. Yep, rawer than this world can even fathom. For being raw is often looked as a flaw, to society's law of wanting all to fit in. For when one is raw, others look at them with mouths hanging to the floorboards as if they had unhinged jaws. For it really be your own at times, some who unwind and thaw themselves to their current state of being and do become raw and alive to the fathers call to be awakened in this day and time. To a lifestyle of having: righteous, assertive awareness, in being wholly wholehearted, to the things of the kingdom of God. Aka raw. For who would want to live a mediocre life when one is called to a life that is raw and adventurous. For this lifestyle is not to be sipped through a straw but to be eaten ravenously, with hands of a relentless hunger to go deep within the father's sea of awareness to the cause. The question that I will leave with you is,

BEARING MY SOUL TO HIM...

"what measures do you think, it will take for you to become raw?"

BEARING MY SOUL TO HIM...

My Delilah

My sweet Delilah. For she is incredibly beautiful. An indescribable work of art that would run a competition with Eve to receive Adam's heart. For she is the one that plays the part in me, in which I often have mistaken her to be my subtle form of flirting; in which I would often catch her earthing and birthing new bottomless turfs within me. For she scares when she comes out to stay for a while. For her own smile is more cunning than the devil's very smile. For if I were to describe her to you, she would have to look like a Greek goddess, that has been created and kissed by Zeus himself. A queen she is, that has been loved by the pharaoh and would kill any man's heart, like a sharp bow and arrow. For she is absurdly beautiful, of which her very existence becomes criminal. For her hair is thick, long, and lush like any lion's mane, to express her loud voice of not wanting to sit still and be tamed and framed in my "never seeing the light of day", hall of fame. For her eyes speaks a thousand games that could never be strained. For her body and skin was kissed by the sun, of which blames and shames me for when others dare to run her obstacle course for fun. For her lip's, cheeks, and eyelids would take on the shade of red rubies, in which sin takes to the stand to sue me; on charges of me asking "isn't this not how a woman should be?" For by the slow flickers of her eyes and signature lip bite, no one dares to stand to fight her with might. For she is my Delilah and that is why I hate her... For do you know the thousands on thousands of men she has turned into samson and has betrayed them? Betraying them as she serves them trays full of their utmost desires and lusts in a one sip drink that turns them to dust. For she is deadlier than any lethal injection, dispelling heartache, and pain as her reaction as she uses such as her currency to indulge in their ever-flowing chalice of sin and despair as her satisfaction. For her forever moment will be plotting against her momentary samson's as she wraps her softer than silk fingers between their hair. Cutting each lock of growth and potential, as they sleep peacefully in her arms of deceit. For her love is a victory, while for you and me it is a defeat. For she is subtle, hard, and cold, like any snake and stone; as she turns her samsons into boulders, like how medusa would turn men into figures of stone. For I do not fear men, for I fear her, of who co-pilots this fleshly body that is my home. For the simple moral of the story is that samson would not be considered as a thrown stone amongst the rubble if he had not met his beloved who had caused him all this trouble. You know the one, Delilah. The same one who sadly lived outside on the doorstep of his home (heart).

BEARING MY SOUL TO HIM...

Games of the heart

Dear abba, I start with my part of the story. For once I actually feel as though this lifestyle isn't quite for me, in which my heart became a player somehow to be apart of the games that play for my heart. For it had seemed as though this ever-growing passion of desiring to be loved by a man genuinely had started from home. In which I questioned it and had phoned home, to only realize that this is where my treasure was supposed to be. A zone that was perfectly made for what I thought was to be for me and my accompanying ego alone. For I just now realized this game of the heart is one deadly weapon, in which it has taken heavens element of love and romance to be that sadistic dart that is cunningly beautiful and yet smart; that has created its own malicious form of art which leaves me including many often running tears and snot. For, I now know the plot. I feel humiliated, robbed, lonely, unattractive, and deprived of love. For this world is so cold that it makes me wonder if it could ever feel the love that is sent from above? As you reply, "oh daughter of mine, do not you know that the games of your heart were already won by me before creation took its first breath." "Walk with me as I bring you to Matthew 10:37 and fly you over the words of John 3:16." "For you are set apart." "For your heart was made and created to hold me only."

"One who is without limit, boundary, nor form; is given unto thee." "As I ask of you to please think clearly as to who instilled within you that never ending abyss of want and attention as I can do all that is beyond your satisfaction." "Do not let your emotions of feeling robbed be your reaction, for you are the gatekeeper that holds the keys to your heart." "Oh, sweet daughter, your only simply feeling a momentary disposition that I feel on a constant bases of my love and heart being taken advantage of." "Do not buckle at the knees when it comes to the games of your heart as it was not made to be played by mortals from the start."

BEARING MY SOUL TO HIM…

Tired of waiting

"For you say that you are tired of waiting and I can see already as your heart is slowing breaking and fading by men who occasionally come to stiff on your beautiful essence away as you become their forever present that will be their momentary past. I know this will come like a shattered glass of unclassed realism. But you are not meant for them. Neither in return are they meant for you. For you see these men as simple frogs who you need to kiss to get your prince. As I assure you these men are not frogs but simple Ishmaels. Ishmaels whose heart is like Esau and intentions are like Cain. I don't blame them as they were only simply taught and maimed by their insane father which teaches them to inflict pain; for pain is their main priority and goal, as you become their victim amongst their inflicted majority; which is served to them as one big soup bowl. For all you need is to wait. Wait on me and I will give him who you seek and have been asking me for, onto thee. As I do remind you that indeed he too needs time. For both of you need to resign your former selves, values, and ways; and let the man and woman of God come forth to me and stay within my safe haven till your length of days. As I am simply asking for you to give me your pail of pain, for you to be set free and that your life can sing yet once again so melodiously unto me.

BEARING MY SOUL TO HIM...

As you can see my beloved, I too am tired in this wired broken-hearted revolver type of reaction, as I only see fit to be the apple of your eye and bring you soul and heart peace, with satisfaction."

BEARING MY SOUL TO HIM...

Being the second option

Dear beloved,

"I guess you now know what it feels like to be the second option. For my loud caution was not on your list of options to choose from, for you to not pursue whatever your heart sets itself upon to do. For I had seen the concoction that enemy had brought into your heart, for you and him to drink on as you allowed him into your home. As you sip back this death and instantly foam at the mouth, as he roams through your veins. Now as you lay there maimed and paralyzed by the numbing inflicted pain: to your choice of subjecting yourself to be, the second option to a man who never had you on his list of options, to begin with. For you were a warily selling yourself as the human auction that you became to be, to gain elements that were never really there as you now see. As I assure you that I know that it might seem unfair, but you are fairer than any rare diamond. For even with this adoption, I too find myself being the second option; to a cause that will knowingly fall into the world's temptations, when being in this fleshly state. As I ask of you to not make the mistake of going to religion to seek refuge for it is a farce and a snake that is sent out on its master's mission to stake out from within, and to have me box in. Essentially by making me be the second option to my flock and kin. So, do not cry or whine my beloved. As I am quite familiar with this broken-hearted contraption. As I ask of you to look at me, as you will never be the second option nor attraction, for my satisfaction."

BEARING MY SOUL TO HIM...

11:59pm

Dear abba,

Somehow, I have become the girl who is only worthy of the 11:59 call. You know the girl only worthy of that nightly appointment check-up. The one who has to stand up and make up her face, body, and mind, for a man who is only erected when he sees her body in a temporary state of his desired disposition. For this is not no rhyme nor fiction, to the unbalanced cause of friction to what lies cunningly beneath the surface of my flesh and the war that is every waking moment waring from within. I know from the beginning that he is not the one. In which your words come sounding again to me like a gong, that is ringing your voice and words; by telling me this isn't your son. Subjecting my beauty and worth to be won of the price of being numb, to be merely something less than who I was called to be. In which you enlighten me, that the one whom I seek is a son of the day; and brings his warmth and rays to bring healing to my hurt and pain. In which you say... "My daughter. Do not take part in the dealings of those sons who Rome by the dome of night." "For their delight is to steal your light, to turn themselves into masters who deceive many and call themselves the abominable light." "For with my given sight, you will discern only that which right and wrong and will desire that which comes out from me who is that light and is known as your home." "So now be made restored in the life that I have given to you." "For you are a daughter of the light, and I will always keep you tight in my arms." "For there is no one that can take you out of my might, for you are only what I delight in." "So, don't believe the lie that you were only worthy for the 11:59 time, as you as more precious than time itself."

BEARING MY SOUL TO HIM...

Reverse pursuer

"Since when did you take the role of being the pursuer? I know your desire of wanting to be a wife and mother is here much sooner than planned to be, but I am here to tell thee this right here is the moment to be free. Free from your heart being stolen but yet won from another in a bond, which goes on beyond, time itself. Free from the mothering role you were met to be, as you cradle your children. Of all kind, close to thee. Free where you and I can only just be. Where I can have you to myself, selfishly for these moments, where you are free, my beloved. For I ask you this question, since when did you take on the role of being a pursuer? For this role was only met for him who seeks thee out, and knows without a doubt that I have set you apart; and placed you within the mount from whence I had told him to find you. For the mount is the place where you and I had run off to, to preserve thee and that nobody could ever get a glimpse of this masterpiece. For the pursuer is I and he who wins thee over and over again. From figures who hold the male designed pursuit, that I have created. I have purposefully made it in order for man to identify what he is been searching for, which is to pursue her. Is it sounding familiar? As you will hear within the word that he was sent and meant to pursue her, for within her, he will find me, the supplier of all his needs. So, take heed my beloved. For, the role of being the pursuer is only meant for him, who is willing to bow his knee and life to save thee."

BEARING MY SOUL TO HIM…

The custody battle

I mean I am shaped and formed in the image of my father. For you might see the resemblance, but in this carbon copy of myself, I cannot seem to help but war with the pestilence that goes on inside my DNA. Can you see it, that I am torn between a custody battle? Clearly, my father and potter had won the battle and now will deprive my enemy like a hunger striven cattle; of me. As you can see though he has won me, my flesh desires to be set free with the other. For the other is giving me an unlimited hot girl summer and perks; but the only bummer that is marked is losing my soul for eternity, for a moment that did not even last for 30mins. You can see even with father I am never left in the state of being bothered, as I adore the father-daughter relationship that we had and more. But yet my flesh is seeking for something abominable, and devilish to be stored as I agree with it at a temporary plea to take the fee to be distant from, he who is my author and finisher of my life story. For I hate the I am sorry, given type of story to thee my father. For you were the martyr, that is always starting with her to be constantly reborn and free from the shackles of an abusive other. That comes to me subtly like a loving brother, that comes with a hug that is only known to make others suffer. As you can see, I am simply a child stuck in between a custody with the father and the other that causes harm and bother. Yes, father has won, and yet I am stuck with the visitation of the other, which awakes the sin within my body to start to stutter. As I only ask in this battle for my heart, it is to not leave me torn apart.

BEARING MY SOUL TO HIM...

His soul is mine

"For I said his soul is mine," saith the lord. "His soul is mine. As you are mine and both of you are thine to one another, as I bind you both together. Let me remind you that he is ultimately mine. For I could not help but find this thing swelling up inside you, that is darker and limitless than time itself. So, with help, I am going to kill this thing that has subtly placed that known blindfold and belt called deceit from around your neck and will repeat these words and say, that his soul is mine. For my daughter, do not take this as if I am speaking to you, for I am commanding that spirit that occasionally peaks it's ugly head from behind you, to drag my son with toys of seductive ploys to destroy him. For I said his soul is mine, and I think it is about time that your deeds be recompensed as I am the recorder of all sinful debts. So, since I am the owner of this house and had not seen any rent from an unwanted pest, you now can go fill out the rest."

BEARING MY SOUL TO HIM…

Own strength

In my strength, I find myself often breaking at patience. For within me patience is never really an option because it brings to me this point of anxiousness. For I know this type of behavior is not us, as children of the most high. For when I am left to patience, I often find myself not being able to touch the sky nor wondering as to why as if I was built to fly in it. In which I often find myself gravitating to the table of my own free will, to dine with my old friends. You know the ones. The triplets of the "me, myself, and I." The twins, Delilah, and Jezebel. Ohm, we cannot forget the conscious to do only that which is hell. Hmm, the couple of "sanity for only vanity." Shackles and boundaries stripped of a title much more a family. Oh, we cannot forget the ever-welcoming host of all abominable things, called the other. As you can see, with all of these present and alive in me I suffer. To doing all things in my strength and not willing to be still as if I receive a temporary thrill of not wanting to be healed. Which often leaves me inches away from being killed, countless of times. As if I never heard this type of rhythmic chime before, to not do things in my strength nor time. In which I momentarily forget, as I whine about my results to my father; in which I know by now it has to be a bother. For it is like I can see it on his lips already, asking if any other of his children are willing to stop her from this never-ending game of Russian roulette, with this type of revolver. As you can see father, nobody including herself can stop her. In which she humbly comes to your feet to bow her body and essence, to admit the defeat and only seeks for you to make her feel complete. As she seeks for your voice, as she knows you are the only one to solve this feeling of always competing. So, to me doing things in my strength with the knowledge that I have, grab hold on to the strength of your father that which is in heaven; for he is more than glad to turn your situation into being unleavened bread.

BEARING MY SOUL TO HIM…

His heart

Today is a new day, that I have come to realize that my knowledge and awareness became alive that I will never be the one to men who are not your son. For I've found that I was only worthy of their temporary form of fun, as I take my place within their stories that they tell their sons; of victories that won over beautiful women as they simplify their beauty and worth to something boringly dumb. Yeah, because I am that one individual that takes things pretty literally. For now, that I see that I was made the girl, only worthy to have their parts but not worthy enough to know or hold their heart from the start. So, to the those out there who find themselves playing the position of some jerks' story of them formerly being horny, to take this as a warning and as a wake-up call as one calls out to another from within the morning. That you have the beauty, worthy, and the stuff to make anyone drop to this earth. As I ask of you to take confidence and pride within the father's guide of birthing new turfs within you, as you subject yourself to be taught by his side. For I know and heard the lie of the enemy's sleigh remarks of such things being hidden from the father's eyes, as we slowly die and become someone's measly temporary form of fun. As if we are called to being toys, subjected to the enemy's ploys to run havoc, fear, and being numb into one's life. Before they meet their destined wife to be. As you can see, this can cause tension and strife within one's life and mind. As I now know that I can say. That I have found that the way to be difficult but yet very pinnacle, and will resign from this former cynical intent; and will fit my will to be bent to his. For as one will find within him is, that he is ultimately worthy of our heart and baggage worries from within.

BEARING MY SOUL TO HIM...

A memory

For my greatest fear is being a simple memory. For a memory takes its place within the temporary, of the temples of who holds its formalities. It has not the mere idea of a memory that has me in fear but my existence taking its place amongst those who were once here. It is merely being the thought of memory to someone else, which suddenly appears and brings with its former emotions as a stacked tier. For my greatest fear is having my legacy forgotten, as my achievements rot away like an untouched fruit, which essence sheds tears for not being consumed. For cannot you see that I do not want my legacy to be looked as a simple memory when they think of me. For I want my legacy to be literally here in the now as if I was yet breathing the breath of life right in through me. The one thing about memory, that I do not fear would be the consistency of its ever reoccurrence of holding its place between time. Like a precious dime, it rolls itself between past, present, future, and time. Even with this poem being rhymed, it is being sketched within the backs of your minds as they take to their place of being simple words that once were mine. So as a sign and a letter to my hopes and dreams of changing this to the pattern of something better, I will sip on your morrows promise father, that will grace me with its presence in the morning like a dove's feather.

BEARING MY SOUL TO HIM...

Failed loyalty

Abba, I have been tainted with failed loyalty. A gruesome reality that has made me a casualty within this war of being known as your family. For failure has soiled me to the point of unrecognition, in my daily diction, which has boiled and scarred your beautiful daughter through toils and sinful morals of ethic portions. For this shame had foiled my pride and big stance, of thinking to myself as immune or untouchable to the world's given demands. I swore that I was stronger, and no longer had the desires of the world left in me. As I only ask for your forgiveness, as I humble my essences so close to the dust of the earth where no man on earth can see me. For my only wish and desire is that you never leave me nor to let your spirit to depart from me; for I am nothing without you. For my parents dedicated me back to you as I do this all the same again, for I refuse to stay paralyzed and lame in my sin. For this body and soul was created to do that which is to do your will, to win and be free from the shackles of sin. For I am calling in advance oh abba, to let me in when I knock at the door; to be restored again. For I am coming to remain permanently at your dining table, until you call on me to give a toast on our wins about life's ploys.

BEARING MY SOUL TO HIM…

BEARING MY SOUL TO HIM...

Lady in waiting

For this goes out to the single ladies out there. You know thy selves in this equation, as I take to the stand to speak of your immediate occasion. For we have become ladies in waiting... For within this delicate process of waiting, we are often left to the ruinous beast of our minds, which constantly leaves us in a state of debating and blind to the father's design. Agreed, as we contemplate the father's promise with those of the uncircumcised heart from the start. For they say, "it's not good for man to be alone." As if we do not get urges too, but hear me my boo; if you merely took the time to look closely at my label that I am both definitively fe-male. Holding the femininity and yet balancing it with the masculinity of my creator's originality. For I too cannot be left to my own devices. As I often trade looks with others, as I sip my glass filled with ice as I battle with isis in these parts of my body. As our elders never really told us how they got over this part of the story as if this patch was old and too boring to tell. Yes, as you can now tell that we may be ladies in waiting, but we are waiting to hear the bridegroom's bell; to come to dwell with him and win.

Toy

Toy with her until you get bored of her. Make it your mission that you lie with her but that you do not die with her. For I want you to lay within the purity of her consciousness, the solidarity of her heart, and for you to depart her emotions like elements that swell to the touch, lastly I want for you to bill her converted will. You know the will she trades with you every-time she extends her hands and her heart for you to receive in order for her to receive that thrill. For I know your name is not bill, but it might as be bill for your only mission is to kill her bill. For I do not need to remind you again of the memo, toy with her until you get bored with her. Make her gravel for more, for she has tasted what we have been plotting and storing for her for years evermore, which is to lure her from her father's arms of warmth.

BEARING MY SOUL TO HIM...

What does it take?

What does it take to win your heart? As one man asks me through text, one day. As if he thought my heart, body, and mind was willing to stay at his given demand. For he said what does it take, to break into your utmost secret places, as he looks at me with anticipation to see if I will do the mistaken to do as he pleases. As he cheeses over my existence with a good riddance, as I become infected with his momentary deliciousness, which then clogs the blood flow to the artery's of my heart, to restrict the God-given love of an ever-flowing abundance to have me set free. As I must say this, to get this off my chest and face this blunt question and sift through it and see that his master calls out to him, to seek my hurt. As my worth can not be simplified, nor watered down, or narrowed down to my words. As I hear my father's voice merge, to purge the vain materialistic sickness that forced my essence and likeness into a box of forsakenness, numbness, and hurt. As if I was worth that. Scratch that, as I will never bat my eye on something that is not fact. As a matter of fact, I will pack that stacked weapon, which was sent from heaven to disassemble that which was mentioned to bring of my enemies' redemption. So, let me get back to the question, what does it take to win your heart. As I will tell thee from now, that was not the smart question to ask from the start. As I will direct thee to go ask the one who formed and had placed the breath of life within thee from the start. As he will tell thee, what it takes.

BEARING MY SOUL TO HIM...

Selfish

Do not ask me why I am selfish. For, I am simply derived by a God who is known to be and hold the title of being jealous. Though I may be selfish. He is selfless, as his knowledge takes root within me, I often fall helpless like Jacobs leg when God had felt this for the first time. For I am selfish and proud, for it comes to my awareness that I once was dead, now made alive and set free and will become who he desires for me to be. For, I have access to a God who is without limit nor boundary. Who ravenously comes to me, just to live inside of me; for others to see that they too can come to dine with us? For within such efforts can you blame me for being selfish on something this perfect. But since I am his servant, who is now made a daughter who is called on to be perfect in him; it gives me this desire to share and to bare a loving warmth that comes from him. For we are wretched and do not deserve it, yet still he is calling for us to come into the throne room of his presence to stay with him; not because we deserve it but because he told us we are worth it.

Sea of broken glass

For if I would have to cross a sea of broken glass on my hands and knees to get to spend a thousand eternity lifetimes with you in utmost bliss; then I would. For I consider my every waking breath a sin against you because let us be honest, I am not worthy to have you. For you are more precious than life it' self and yet my essence can't help but fathom the abomination of itself to be mirrored in the likeness of such perfection. For by your resurrection I was given another direction for redemption. For all my existence can say or mumble is I am sorry. For let me demonstrate my apology by crossing a sea of broken glass on my hands and knees to you. For all the times, I have demonstrated actions that had seemed as though I was purposely hating you or was against you. For its not you that I hate, or I toil with daily but this ever-companioning ego of sin which lashes out against you, is what I fight against as I cross this sea of broken glass to you. For you are worth every sliver of glass and every drop of my blood to be shed for you because let us be blunt, you did it for me too…

BEARING MY SOUL TO HIM…

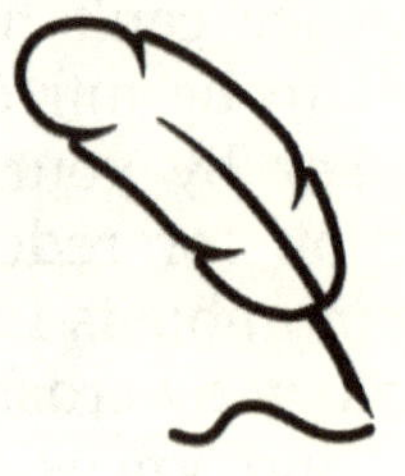